better together*

*This book is best read together, grownup and kid.

a kids book about™

a kids book about™ systemic racism

by Jordan Thierry

a kids book about™

Printed in the United States of America

Library of Congress cataloging available.

A Kids Book About books are exclusively available online on the A Kids Book About website.

To share your stories, ask questions, or inquire about bulk purchases (schools, libraries, and nonprofits), please use the following email address:

hello@akidsbookabout.com

www.akidsbookabout.com

ISBN: 978-1-951253-45-5

For Carver and Ischer.

Intro

Despite the reality that the majority of people today likely agree with the words in the "I Have a Dream" speech by Dr. Martin Luther King Jr., we're living in a moment where racial injustice, implicit bias, and inequality continue to thrive. Systemic racism helps explain why this is.

No matter when you're reading this, or where in the world you may be, this book is relevant. It will remain relevant because racism can't be undone in one generation. This book is designed to help you start a conversation with the next generation. To help them understand and begin to see where and how racism continues to persist, save them from the confusion we've experienced, and prepare them to want to do something about it.

This is a book about
systemic racism.

And believe it or not,
it's actually for kids.

I have to say,
this book was really
hard to write.

Systemic racism
is incredibly difficult
to understand...

even for grownups!

But to help
make sense of it,

I'm going to start
with an example.

I'm Black.

Did you know that it's really rare for someone with my skin color to write a kids book?

When I was a kid,
I almost never
read a book by a
Black author.

That might seem normal
or like no big deal...

but it shouldn't be normal.

And it is a big deal.

But that's how it works...

Systemic racism

SEE

EMS

normal.

It's almost like
it's invisible.

Something that's always around, but you never quite see it...

unless you look really hard.

So my hope with
this kids book is to help
you not only see it...

but want to do
something about it.

You might already know
what racism is.

It's when
someone is excluded,
treated badly, or hated
because of their race
or skin color.

Systemic racism
is when racist ideas
are built into laws,
schools, stories,
and other institutions
in a way that
collectively makes
life much harder for
people of color.

Let me give you some
more examples.

When I was a kid, the only people on TV that looked like me were athletes, comedians, or rappers.

When I was in school, I was suspended for things that my white friends often were not.

When I was in class, I never had a teacher that looked like me until I went to college.

When I was a teenager,
I was stopped by the police
multiple times, while many of
my white friends weren't.

Looking at these moments, it may not seem like it was about the color of my skin.

But systemic racism isn't always obvious, which is what makes it so hard to see.

Before I understood that, I use to get frustrated and angry.

Even at myself.

But as I grew up, I noticed I wasn't the only one experiencing this.

Other people of color were experiencing the same things.

That's when
I started to notice a

patt

tern

I learned that if
you're Black...

You're more likely to
be stopped by the police.

It can be harder to get a job.

It can be more difficult
to buy a home.

You're less likely to go
to a good school.

You're less likely
to be in charge.

And most heroes in stories
don't look like you.

As you read these things,

you might feel sad...

or even angry.

You also might start
to wonder how it got
this way.

Well, the reason is
long and complicated,

but I'll do my best to explain.

Since the start of our
country,* many people
with white skin whose families
came from Europe were
given land, opportunity,
and access to money...

*The United States of America.

While people of color—those with black and brown skin and the Indigenous people that lived on the land before white people arrived—were attacked, killed, and sold into slavery.

Lies were told about people of color to scare white people.

To make white people believe that people of color would hurt them, steal their property, or give them diseases.

Yes, really.

SADLY, MANY PEOPLE BELIEVED THOSE LIES.

Then, even after they fought for their freedom, people of color still didn't have as many rights. They still had more obstacles and experienced a lot of discrimination.

New laws were even created to make life harder for them because many white people didn't want to share.

Over time, the value
of land and money increased,
which gave white people
more and more for their kids,
grandkids, and so on.

Today,
this unequal balance
of who has

land,

money,

power,

and rights

still exists and affects
people of color.

It affects their ability to live in nice homes and neighborhoods.

It affects their ability to start their own businesses and donate their money to good causes.

It affects the amount of money that is put into building schools and hiring great teachers.

It affects their ability to speak their own languages and preserve their cultures.

It affects their ability to tell their own stories or make their own TV shows and movies.

It affects who has access to medicine and good doctors.

It affects how they are treated by the police, government, and court system.

All of these things are the result of systemic racism.

And even though people
of color have more equality
today than they ever have...

new forms of systemic racism are created all the time.

We need to change the system and erase the racist ideas that live in our laws, schools, stories, and other institutions. We need to create ways for people of color—

who have been left behind for so long—to catch up so that money, land, great schools, quality doctors, and basic rights are equally available to everyone.

Systemic racism
isn't new.

It's just hard to see.

But once you do—it's
hard to ignore.

So practice seeing systemic racism every day.

In the schools you go to.
Movies you watch.
Neighborhood you live in.
Point it out to your friends.
Point it out to your family.

Because systemic racism can't be undone until we open our eyes and see it.

Outro

Now that you've made it to the end of the book, what's next?

Well, this will likely just be the beginning of a series of conversations about systemic racism and racial injustice. I bet your kiddo will have a lot of questions over the next few weeks. They may even point things out to you and ask, "Is that because of systemic racism?" You may not have all the answers and that's OK.

It's important to be honest and let children know that adults are still learning about systemic racism and trying to address it as well. However, if you want to feel more confident in talking about systemic racism and start answering some of those questions, try doing some "adult reading" on it. Native American history and Black history is a great place to start. Take advantage of this opportunity to show your kiddos that you're still learning, and this is a topic that you will continue to learn about together.

find more kids books about

white privilege, emotions, gender, autism, community, adoption, belonging, shame, empathy, gratitude, and mindfulness.

 akidsbookabout.com

share your read*

*Tell somebody, post a photo, or give this book away to share what you care about.

@akidsbookabout